the NLT
BIBLE
PROMISE
BOOK

Tyndale House Publishers, Inc., Carol Stream, Illinois

Visit Tyndale online at www.tyndale.com and www.newlivingtranslation.com.

TYNDALE, New Living Translation, NLT, the New Living Translation logo, and Tyndale's quill logo are registered trademarks of Tyndale House Publishers, Inc.

The NLT Bible Promise Book

Copyright © 2007 by Ron Beers. All rights reserved.

Cover photograph of hummingbird © Carlos Luis Camacho Photographs/ Getty Images. All rights reserved.

Designed by Julie Chen

Compiled and edited by Amy E. Mason. All rights reserved.

Scripture quotations are taken from the *Holy Bible,* New Living Translation, copyright © 1996, 2004, 2007 by Tyndale House Foundation. Used by permission of Tyndale House Publishers, Inc., Carol Stream, Illinois 60188. All rights reserved.

ISBN 978-1-4143-1356-6

Repackage first published in 2012 under ISBN 978-1-4143-6984-6.

Printed in the United States of America

18
8

CONTENTS

Small things often have a great impact. This pocket book of Bible promises is small in size, but we hope it will become one of your most treasured resources for hope and encouragement. Life is full of twists and surprises—some good and some bad. As we try to live day by day, month by month, and year by year, we face many hurts, doubts, and problems. We have many questions about what to do next, where to go, and why things happen the way they do. Life doesn't always work according to plan. So how do we keep moving forward with a positive attitude, hope, and a spirit of joy in spite of the bumps along the way? This little book can help you make sense of today's challenges because it is filled with God's promises. Knowing God's promises helps life make sense and gives you a confident peace and security in the midst of confusing and chaotic circumstances. When you have questions, doubts, or fears, this book can be a wonderful resource to come back to again and again.

Thankfully, God keeps all his promises. This makes his Word, the Bible, the greatest of treasures, because it is filled with promises you know will be kept. These are promises God makes not only to his people in general but to you personally. One of God's greatest promises is that his Word will last forever (Isaiah 40:8; Matthew 24:35; 1 Peter 1:23-25), which means his promises will also stand for eternity. Though human promises often fail and disappoint us, God's promises fulfill and sustain us by providing guidance, teaching, encouragement, forgiveness, joy, and the confidence that the future is secure.

This little book is full of God's greatest and most personal promises—more than 375 promises covering ninety different topics. All the promises are drawn from the New Living Translation, the most readable and accurate translation available today. The topics selected in this book cover different times and different walks of life to show that God's care and concern extend to all people for all time, including you! His promises are relevant in your most needy hour, as well as in your times of blessing and in the routine of everyday life. Knowing God's promises will help you discover what God desires for your life and how to receive and enjoy all that God has in store for you.

@ ACCEPTANCE

When you need to feel accepted by God . . .

Even if my father and mother abandon me, the LORD will
hold me close.
Psalm 27:10

Since we have been made right in God's sight by faith, we
have peace with God because of what Jesus Christ our Lord
has done for us. Because of our faith, Christ has brought us
into this place of undeserved privilege where we now stand,
and we confidently and joyfully look forward to sharing
God's glory.
Romans 5:1-2

Nothing in all creation will ever be able to separate us from
the love of God that is revealed in Christ Jesus our Lord.
Romans 8:39

When you're having trouble accepting life's circumstances . . .

To enjoy your work and accept your lot in life—this is indeed a gift from God.
  Ecclesiastes 5:19

You will keep in perfect peace all who trust in you, all whose thoughts are fixed on you!
  Isaiah 26:3

You suffered along with those who were thrown into jail, and when all you owned was taken from you, you accepted it with joy. You knew there were better things waiting for you that will last forever.
  Hebrews 10:34

ANGELS

When you wonder how angels are involved in the world today . . .

The angel of the LORD is a guard; he surrounds and defends all who fear him.
  Psalm 34:7

Don't forget to show hospitality to strangers, for some who have done this have entertained angels without realizing it!
  Hebrews 13:2

ANGER

When you're feeling angry at others . . .

If you are even angry with someone, you are subject to judgment!
Matthew 5:22

Dear friends, never take revenge. Leave that to the righteous anger of God. For the Scriptures say, "I will take revenge; I will pay them back," says the LORD.
Romans 12:19

"Don't sin by letting anger control you." Don't let the sun go down while you are still angry, for anger gives a foothold to the devil.
Ephesians 4:26-27

When you're afraid God is angry with you . . .

You are a God of forgiveness, gracious and merciful, slow to become angry, and rich in unfailing love.
Nehemiah 9:17

His anger lasts only a moment, but his favor lasts a lifetime! Weeping may last through the night, but joy comes with the morning.
Psalm 30:5

BEGINNINGS

When you feel the need to start over . . .

Great is his faithfulness; his mercies begin afresh each morning.
  Lamentations 3:23

Anyone who belongs to Christ has become a new person.
The old life is gone; a new life has begun!
  2 Corinthians 5:17

BELIEF

When you feel lost and don't know what to believe in . . .

I have come as a light to shine in this dark world, so that all
who put their trust in me will no longer remain in the dark.
  John 12:46

When you question whether simply believing is enough . . .

I tell you the truth, anyone who believes has eternal life.
  John 6:47

Believe in the Lord Jesus and you will be saved.
  Acts 16:31

When you question the power of belief in God . . .

"What do you mean, 'If I can'?" Jesus asked. "Anything is
possible if a person believes."
  Mark 9:23

When you want to experience God's blessings . . .

How great is the goodness you have stored up for those who fear you. You lavish it on those who come to you for protection, blessing them before the watching world.
   Psalm 31:19

Blessed are those who trust in the LORD and have made the LORD their hope and confidence.
   Jeremiah 17:7

When you wonder about the blessings that come from obeying God . . .

Oh, the joys of those who do not follow the advice of the wicked.
   Psalm 1:1

How great is the goodness you have stored up for those who fear you. You lavish it on those who come to you for protection, blessing them before the watching world.
   Psalm 31:19

The LORD will withhold no good thing from those who do what is right.
   Psalm 84:11

CHANGE

When you're looking for stability in the midst of change . . .

The grass withers and the flowers fade, but the word of our God stands forever.
Isaiah 40:8

I am the LORD, and I do not change.
Malachi 3:6

When you need to make a change . . .

Don't copy the behavior and customs of this world, but let God transform you into a new person by changing the way you think. Then you will learn to know God's will for you, which is good and pleasing and perfect.
Romans 12:2

COMFORT

When it seems there is no one to comfort you . . .

Even when I walk through the darkest valley, I will not be afraid, for you are close beside me. Your rod and your staff protect and comfort me.
Psalm 23:4

The LORD is close to the brokenhearted.
Psalm 34:18

When you need someone who understands you . . .

In all their suffering he also suffered, and he personally rescued them. In his love and mercy he redeemed them. He lifted them up and carried them through all the years.
  Isaiah 63:9

When you're seeking words of comfort . . .

I meditate on your age-old regulations; O Lord, they comfort me.
  Psalm 119:52

When you need to sympathize with others . . .

God is our merciful Father and the source of all comfort. He comforts us in all our troubles so that we can comfort others. When they are troubled, we will be able to give them the same comfort God has given us.
  2 Corinthians 1:3-4

CONSEQUENCES

When you want to know the importance of righteous living . . .

Plant the good seeds of righteousness, and you will harvest a crop of love. Plow up the hard ground of your hearts, for now is the time to seek the Lord, that he may come and shower righteousness upon you.
  Hosea 10:12

When you feel you can never escape the consequences of your sins . . .

Obey me, and I will be your God, and you will be my people. Do everything as I say, and all will be well!
  Jeremiah 7:23

Anyone who belongs to Christ has become a new person. The old life is gone; a new life has begun!
  2 Corinthians 5:17

CONTENTMENT

When you're feeling dissatisfied . . .

Enjoy what you have rather than desiring what you don't have. Just dreaming about nice things is meaningless— like chasing the wind.
  Ecclesiastes 6:9

I have learned how to be content with whatever I have. I know how to live on almost nothing or with everything. I have learned the secret of living in every situation, whether it is with a full stomach or empty, with plenty or little. For I can do everything through Christ, who gives me strength.
  Philippians 4:11-13

Don't love money; be satisfied with what you have. For God has said, "I will never fail you. I will never abandon you."
  Hebrews 13:5

COURAGE

When you need to be brave . . .

This is my command—be strong and courageous! Do not be afraid or discouraged. For the LORD your God is with you wherever you go.
> *Joshua 1:9*

Don't be afraid, for I am with you. Don't be discouraged, for I am your God. I will strengthen you and help you. I will hold you up with my victorious right hand.
> *Isaiah 41:10*

When you need to speak boldly about your faith . . .

When you are brought to trial in the synagogues and before rulers and authorities, don't worry about how to defend yourself or what to say, for the Holy Spirit will teach you at that time what needs to be said.
> *Luke 12:11-12*

DEATH

When you're afraid of death . . .

Even when I walk through the darkest valley, I will not be afraid, for you are close beside me.
> *Psalm 23:4*

My health may fail, and my spirit may grow weak, but God remains the strength of my heart; he is mine forever.

Psalm 73:26

Don't be afraid of those who want to kill your body; they cannot touch your soul.

Matthew 10:28

When you want to know what happens when you die . . .

I am the resurrection and the life. Anyone who believes in me will live, even after dying.

John 11:25

The wages of sin is death, but the free gift of God is eternal life through Christ Jesus our Lord.

Romans 6:23

DECISIONS

When you're facing big life choices . . .

Show me the right path, O LORD; point out the road for me to follow. . . . Who are those who fear the LORD? He will show them the path they should choose.

Psalm 25:4, 12

Commit everything you do to the LORD. Trust him, and he will help you.

Psalm 37:5

When you're having trouble sticking to what you've decided . . .

I have chosen to be faithful; I have determined to live by your regulations.
Psalm 119:30

Let's not get tired of doing what is good. At just the right time we will reap a harvest of blessing if we don't give up.
Galatians 6:9

When your bad choices come back to haunt you . . .

When people do not accept divine guidance, they run wild. But whoever obeys the law is joyful.
Proverbs 29:18

Come back to the place of safety, all you prisoners who still have hope! I promise this very day that I will repay two blessings for each of your troubles.
Zechariah 9:12

DEPRESSION

When your circumstances seem hopeless . . .

I know the LORD is always with me. I will not be shaken, for he is right beside me. No wonder my heart is glad, and I rejoice. My body rests in safety. . . . You will show me the way of life, granting me the joy of your presence and the pleasures of living with you forever.
Psalm 16:8-9, 11

Even though the fig trees have no blossoms, and there are no grapes on the vines; even though the olive crop fails, and the fields lie empty and barren; even though the flocks die in the fields, and the cattle barns are empty, yet I will rejoice in the LORD! I will be joyful in the God of my salvation!
Habakkuk 3:17-18

When you feel you can't fight the sadness . . .

The LORD is close to the brokenhearted; he rescues those whose spirits are crushed.
Psalm 34:18

He lifted me out of the pit of despair.
Psalm 40:2

Why am I discouraged? Why is my heart so sad? I will put my hope in God! I will praise him again—my Savior and my God!
Psalm 42:5-6

DESIRES

When you're seeking the things that God wants for you . . .

Take delight in the LORD, and he will give you your heart's desires. Commit everything you do to the LORD. Trust him, and he will help you.
Psalm 37:4-5

When you find yourself chasing after the wrong desires . . .

I will give you a new heart, and I will put a new spirit in you. I will take out your stony, stubborn heart and give you a tender, responsive heart.
Ezekiel 36:26

When you follow the desires of your sinful nature, the results are very clear: sexual immorality, impurity, lustful pleasures, idolatry, sorcery, hostility, quarreling, jealousy, outbursts of anger, selfish ambition, dissension, division, envy, drunkenness, wild parties, and other sins like these. Let me tell you again, as I have before, that anyone living that sort of life will not inherit the Kingdom of God.
Galatians 5:19-21

DOUBT

When you're feeling uncertain about God . . .

Blessed are those who trust in the LORD and have made the LORD their hope and confidence.
Jeremiah 17:7

We are always confident . . . for we live by believing and not by seeing.
2 Corinthians 5:6-7

When you lose confidence in yourself . . .

I tell you the truth, if you have faith and don't doubt, you can do things like this and much more. You can even say to this mountain, "May you be lifted up and thrown into the sea," and it will happen. You can pray for anything, and if you have faith, you will receive it.
   Matthew 21:21-22

ENCOURAGEMENT

When you're feeling discouraged . . .

Let's not get tired of doing what is good. At just the right time we will reap a harvest of blessing if we don't give up.
   Galatians 6:9

In his kindness God called you to share in his eternal glory by means of Christ Jesus. So after you have suffered a little while, he will restore, support, and strengthen you, and he will place you on a firm foundation.
   1 Peter 5:10

When you just need to lift your spirits . . .

The joy of the LORD is your strength!
   Nehemiah 8:10

As soon as I pray, you answer me; you encourage me by giving me strength.
   Psalm 138:3

The Scriptures give us hope and encouragement as we wait patiently for God's promises to be fulfilled.
Romans 15:4

ETERNITY/ETERNAL LIFE

When you doubt there is life after death . . .

Those who die in the LORD will live; their bodies will rise again! Those who sleep in the earth will rise up and sing for joy! For your life-giving light will fall like dew on your people in the place of the dead!
Isaiah 26:19

God loved the world so much that he gave his one and only Son, so that everyone who believes in him will not perish but have eternal life.
John 3:16

When you're wondering how to live with an eternal perspective . . .

We know that God causes everything to work together for the good of those who love God and are called according to his purpose for them.
Romans 8:28

These trials will show that your faith is genuine. It is being tested as fire tests and purifies gold—though your faith is far more precious than mere gold. So when your faith remains strong through many trials, it will bring you much praise and glory and honor on the day when Jesus Christ is revealed to the whole world.

1 Peter 1:7

FAILURE

When you've messed up . . .

The LORD directs the steps of the godly. He delights in every detail of their lives. Though they stumble, they will never fall, for the LORD holds them by the hand.

Psalm 37:23-24

When you're feeling inadequate . . .

How precious are your thoughts about me, O God.

Psalm 139:17

Not a single sparrow can fall to the ground without your Father knowing it. And the very hairs on your head are all numbered. So don't be afraid; you are more valuable to God than a whole flock of sparrows.

Matthew 10:29-31

God has not given us a spirit of fear and timidity, but of power, love, and self-discipline.

2 Timothy 1:7

When you're ready to try again . . .

I focus on this one thing: Forgetting the past and looking
forward to what lies ahead, I press on to reach the end of the
race and receive the heavenly prize for which God, through
Christ Jesus, is calling us.
Philippians 3:13-14

FAITH

When you're wondering what to have faith in . . .

Believe in the Lord Jesus and you will be saved.
Acts 16:31

When you're wondering why faith is important . . .

Faith is the confidence that what we hope for will actually
happen; it gives us assurance about things we cannot see.
Hebrews 11:1

It is impossible to please God without faith. Anyone who
wants to come to him must believe that God exists and that
he rewards those who sincerely seek him.
Hebrews 11:6

When you want to strengthen your faith . . .

Let your roots grow down into him, and let your lives be built
on him. Then your faith will grow strong in the truth you
were taught, and you will overflow with thankfulness.
Colossians 2:7

When your faith remains strong through many trials, it will bring you much praise and glory and honor on the day when Jesus Christ is revealed to the whole world.

1 Peter 1:7

When you have faith in God . . .

Have faith in God. I tell you the truth, you can say to this mountain, "May you be lifted up and thrown into the sea," and it will happen. But you must really believe it will happen and have no doubt in your heart.

Mark 11:22-23

Blessed are those who believe without seeing me.

John 20:29

FAITHFULNESS

When you question God's faithfulness . . .

God is not a man, so he does not lie. He is not human, so he does not change his mind. Has he ever spoken and failed to act? Has he ever promised and not carried it through?

Numbers 23:19

The love of the LORD remains forever with those who fear him. His salvation extends to the children's children of those who are faithful to his covenant, of those who obey his commandments!

Psalm 103:17-18

Let us hold tightly without wavering to the hope we affirm, for God can be trusted to keep his promise.
Hebrews 10:23

When you've been unfaithful to God . . .

Great is his faithfulness; his mercies begin afresh each morning.
Lamentations 3:23

If we are unfaithful, he remains faithful, for he cannot deny who he is.
2 Timothy 2:13

⚬ FEAR

When your worst fears come true . . .

When you go through deep waters, I will be with you. When you go through rivers of difficulty, you will not drown. When you walk through the fire of oppression, you will not be burned up; the flames will not consume you.
Isaiah 43:2

We can say with confidence, "The LORD is my helper, so I will have no fear. What can mere people do to me?"
Hebrews 13:6

When you're in danger . . .

The LORD is my light and my salvation—so why should I be afraid? The LORD is my fortress, protecting me from danger, so why should I tremble? . . . Though a mighty army surrounds me, my heart will not be afraid. Even if I am attacked, I will remain confident.

Psalm 27:1, 3

When you're feeling alone and vulnerable . . .

Don't be afraid, for I am with you. Don't be discouraged, for I am your God. I will strengthen you and help you. I will hold you up with my victorious right hand.

Isaiah 41:10

I am convinced that nothing can ever separate us from God's love. Neither death nor life, neither angels nor demons, neither our fears for today nor our worries about tomorrow— not even the powers of hell can separate us from God's love.

Romans 8:38

When you must confront your fears . . .

See, God has come to save me. I will trust in him and not be afraid. The LORD GOD is my strength and my song; he has given me victory.

Isaiah 12:2

FORGIVENESS

When you're seeking God's forgiveness . . .

If we confess our sins to him, he is faithful and just to forgive us our sins and to cleanse us from all wickedness.
1 John 1:9

When you feel your sins are too horrible and too many to forgive . . .

The LORD is slow to anger and filled with unfailing love, forgiving every kind of sin and rebellion.
Numbers 14:18

Though your sins are like scarlet, I will make them as white as snow.
Isaiah 1:18

I—yes, I alone—will blot out your sins for my own sake and will never think of them again.
Isaiah 43:25

When you need to forgive someone else . . .

When you are praying, first forgive anyone you are holding a grudge against, so that your Father in heaven will forgive your sins, too.
Mark 11:25

Make allowance for each other's faults, and forgive anyone who offends you. Remember, the Lord forgave you, so you must forgive others.
Colossians 3:13

FREEDOM

When you're feeling trapped in a sinful way of life . . .

I will say to the prisoners, "Come out in freedom."
Isaiah 49:9

Sin is no longer your master, for you no longer live under the requirements of the law. Instead, you live under the freedom of God's grace.
Romans 6:14

The Scriptures declare that we are all prisoners of sin, so we receive God's promise of freedom only by believing in Jesus Christ.
Galatians 3:22

FRUITFULNESS

When you want to be used by God to accomplish his work . . .

The godly will flourish like palm trees and grow strong like the cedars of Lebanon. For they are transplanted to the LORD's own house. They flourish in the courts of our God. Even in old age they will still produce fruit; they will remain vital and green.
Psalm 92:12-14

I am the vine; you are the branches. Those who remain in me, and I in them, will produce much fruit.
John 15:5

FUTURE

When you're worried about the future . . .

"I know the plans I have for you," says the LORD. "They are plans for good and not for disaster, to give you a future and a hope."
  Jeremiah 29:11

Don't worry about tomorrow, for tomorrow will bring its own worries. Today's trouble is enough for today.
  Matthew 6:34

When you're planning for the future . . .

The LORD says, "I will guide you along the best pathway for your life. I will advise you and watch over you."
  Psalm 32:8

You guide me with your counsel, leading me to a glorious destiny.
  Psalm 73:24

GIVING

When you're deciding how much to give . . .

Give, and you will receive. Your gift will return to you in full—pressed down, shaken together to make room for more, running over, and poured into your lap. The amount you give will determine the amount you get back.
  Luke 6:38

You must each decide in your heart how much to give. And don't give reluctantly or in response to pressure. "For God loves a person who gives cheerfully." And God will generously provide all you need. Then you will always have everything you need and plenty left over to share with others.

2 Corinthians 9:7-8

When you feel you have nothing to offer . . .

Feed the hungry, and help those in trouble. Then your light will shine out from the darkness, and the darkness around you will be as bright as noon.

Isaiah 58:10

If you give even a cup of cold water to one of the least of my followers, you will surely be rewarded.

Matthew 10:42

GOSSIP

When other people are spreading lies about you . . .

He will send help from heaven to rescue me, disgracing those who hound me.

Psalm 57:3

God blesses you when people mock you and persecute you and lie about you and say all sorts of evil things against you because you are my followers. . . . A great reward awaits you in heaven.

Matthew 5:11-12

When you're tempted to gossip . . .

Does anyone want to live a life that is long and prosperous?
Then keep your tongue from speaking evil and your lips from
telling lies!
  Psalm 34:12-13

GRIEF

When you've lost someone you love . . .

He will swallow up death forever! The Sovereign LORD will
wipe away all tears.
  Isaiah 25:8

God blesses those who mourn, for they will be comforted.
  Matthew 5:4

When you're brokenhearted . . .

I will be glad and rejoice in your unfailing love, for you have
seen my troubles, and you care about the anguish of my soul.
  Psalm 31:7

The LORD is close to the brokenhearted; he rescues those
whose spirits are crushed.
  Psalm 34:18

GROWTH

When you want to mature in your faith . . .

The righteous keep moving forward, and those with clean hands become stronger and stronger.
Job 17:9

We ask God to give you complete knowledge of his will and to give you spiritual wisdom and understanding. Then the way you live will always honor and please the Lord, and your lives will produce every kind of good fruit. All the while, you will grow as you learn to know God better and better.
Colossians 1:9-10

Christ will make his home in your hearts as you trust in him. Your roots will grow down into God's love and keep you strong.
Ephesians 3:17

I am certain that God, who began the good work within you, will continue his work until it is finally finished on the day when Christ Jesus returns.
Philippians 1:6

GUIDANCE

When you don't know what to do . . .

If you need wisdom, ask our generous God, and he will give it to you. He will not rebuke you for asking. But when you ask him, be sure that your faith is in God alone. Do not waver, for a person with divided loyalty is as unsettled as a wave of the sea that is blown and tossed by the wind.

James 1:5-6

When you're looking for direction in life . . .

The LORD directs the steps of the godly. He delights in every detail of their lives.

Psalm 37:23

Seek his will in all you do, and he will show you which path to take.

Proverbs 3:6

GUILT

When you're ashamed of your past . . .

Purify me from my sins, and I will be clean; wash me, and I will be whiter than snow.

Psalm 51:7

He has removed our sins as far from us as the east is from the west.

Psalm 103:12

Anyone who belongs to Christ has become a new person. The old life is gone; a new life has begun!

2 Corinthians 5:17

Even if we feel guilty, God is greater than our feelings, and he knows everything.

1 John 3:20

When others condemn you . . .

Those who look to him for help will be radiant with joy; no shadow of shame will darken their faces.

Psalm 34:5

Everyone has sinned; we all fall short of God's glorious standard. Yet God, with undeserved kindness, declares that we are righteous. He did this through Christ Jesus when he freed us from the penalty for our sins.

Romans 3:23-24

HEAVEN

When you're wondering what heaven will be like . . .

I heard a loud shout from the throne, saying, "Look, God's home is now among his people! He will live with them, and they will be his people. God himself will be with them. He will wipe every tear from their eyes, and there will be no more death or sorrow or crying or pain. All these things are gone forever."

Revelation 21:3-4

The holy city . . . shone with the glory of God and sparkled like a precious stone—like jasper as clear as crystal. . . . The wall was made of jasper, and the city was pure gold, as clear as glass. The wall of the city was built on foundation stones inlaid with twelve precious stones. . . . The twelve gates were made of pearls—each gate from a single pearl! And the main street was pure gold, as clear as glass.

Revelation 21:10-11, 18-19, 21

The city has no need of sun or moon, for the glory of God illuminates the city, and the Lamb is its light. . . . Its gates will never be closed at the end of day because there is no night there.

Revelation 21:23, 25

When you're wondering if you will go to heaven . . .

I tell you the truth, anyone who believes has eternal life.

John 6:47

Those who live only to satisfy their own sinful nature will harvest decay and death from that sinful nature. But those who live to please the Spirit will harvest everlasting life from the Spirit.

Galatians 6:8

✤ HELP

When you feel alone with no one to help you . . .

He has not ignored or belittled the suffering of the needy.
He has not turned his back on them, but has listened to their
cries for help.
Psalm 22:24

Commit everything you do to the LORD. Trust him, and he
will help you.
Psalm 37:5

The LORD helps the fallen and lifts those bent beneath their
loads.
Psalm 145:14

When you think you can do it without God . . .

Remain in me, and I will remain in you. For a branch cannot
produce fruit if it is severed from the vine, and you cannot be
fruitful unless you remain in me. Yes, I am the vine; you are
the branches. Those who remain in me, and I in them, will
produce much fruit. For apart from me you can do nothing.
John 15:4-5

When you experience God's divine care for you . . .

Let all who take refuge in you rejoice; let them sing joyful
praises forever. Spread your protection over them, that all who
love your name may be filled with joy.
Psalm 5:11

HOLY SPIRIT

When you need supernatural comfort . . .

The Holy Spirit helps us in our weakness. For example, we don't know what God wants us to pray for. But the Holy Spirit prays for us with groanings that cannot be expressed in words. And the Father who knows all hearts knows what the Spirit is saying, for the Spirit pleads for us believers in harmony with God's own will.
   Romans 8:26-27

When you need the personal presence of God . . .

We have received God's Spirit (not the world's spirit), so we can know the wonderful things God has freely given us.
   1 Corinthians 2:12

Those who obey God's commandments remain in fellowship with him, and he with them. And we know he lives in us because the Spirit he gave us lives in us.
   1 John 3:24

HONESTY

When it's hard to be honest . . .

May integrity and honesty protect me, for I put my hope in you.
   Psalm 25:21

What joy for those whose record the LORD has cleared of guilt, whose lives are lived in complete honesty!
  Psalm 32:2

Honesty guides good people; dishonesty destroys treacherous people. . . . The godly are directed by honesty; the wicked fall beneath their load of sin.
  Proverbs 11:3, 5

When you're tempted to lie . . .

Truthful words stand the test of time, but lies are soon exposed.
  Proverbs 12:19

Don't lie to each other, for you have stripped off your old sinful nature and all its wicked deeds. Put on your new nature, and be renewed as you learn to know your Creator and become like him.
  Colossians 3:9-10

HOPE

When you feel like giving up . . .

When doubts filled my mind, your comfort gave me renewed hope and cheer.
  Psalm 94:19

"I know the plans I have for you," says the LORD. "They are plans for good and not for disaster, to give you a future and a hope."
  Jeremiah 29:11

When you're wondering if there is anything to hope for . . .

Hope in the LORD; for with the LORD there is unfailing love. His redemption overflows.
  Psalm 130:7

This is the secret: Christ lives in you. This gives you assurance of sharing his glory.
  Colossians 1:27

HUMILITY

When you want to be the greatest . . .

Anyone who becomes as humble as this little child is the greatest in the Kingdom of Heaven.
  Matthew 18:4

When you think you deserve all the credit . . .

He leads the humble in doing right, teaching them his way.
  Psalm 25:9

Though the LORD is great, he cares for the humble, but he keeps his distance from the proud.
  Psalm 138:6

I live in the high and holy place with those whose spirits are contrite and humble. I restore the crushed spirit of the humble and revive the courage of those with repentant hearts.
  Isaiah 57:15

When you wonder if humility will get you anywhere . . .

True humility and fear of the LORD lead to riches, honor, and long life.

Proverbs 22:4

IMPOSSIBILITY

When it seems the odds are against you . . .

Nothing is impossible with God.

Luke 1:37

All glory to God, who is able, through his mighty power at work within us, to accomplish infinitely more than we might ask or think.

Ephesians 3:20

When you wonder if anything is impossible for God . . .

God has given both his promise and his oath. These two things are unchangeable because it is impossible for God to lie. Therefore, we who have fled to him for refuge can have great confidence as we hold to the hope that lies before us.

Hebrews 6:18

INJUSTICE

When things don't seem fair . . .

Those who plant injustice will harvest disaster, and their reign of terror will come to an end. Blessed are those who are generous, because they feed the poor.
Proverbs 22:8-9

God will use this persecution to show his justice and to make you worthy of his Kingdom, for which you are suffering. In his justice he will pay back those who persecute you.
2 Thessalonians 1:5-6

JEALOUSY

When you find yourself desiring what someone else has . . .

Most people are motivated to success because they envy their neighbors. But this, too, is meaningless—like chasing the wind.
Ecclesiastes 4:4

Wherever there is jealousy and selfish ambition, there you will find disorder and evil of every kind.
James 3:16

When you want to be like someone else . . .

Don't envy sinners, but always continue to fear the LORD. You will be rewarded for this; your hope will not be disappointed.
Proverbs 23:17-18

Those who belong to Christ Jesus have nailed the passions and desires of their sinful nature to his cross and crucified them there. Since we are living by the Spirit, let us follow the Spirit's leading in every part of our lives. Let us not become conceited, or provoke one another, or be jealous of one another.

Galatians 5:24-26

JESUS CHRIST

When you want to belong to someone . . .

Where two or three gather together as my followers, I am there among them.

Matthew 18:20

God loved the world so much that he gave his one and only Son, so that everyone who believes in him will not perish but have eternal life. God sent his Son into the world not to judge the world, but to save the world through him.

John 3:16-17

When you wonder whether Christ can help . . .

I can do everything through Christ, who gives me strength.

Philippians 4:13

He existed before anything else, and he holds all creation together.

Colossians 1:17

When you need to hear good news . . .

God promised this Good News long ago through his prophets in the holy Scriptures. The Good News is about his Son. In his earthly life he was born into King David's family line, and he was shown to be the Son of God when he was raised from the dead by the power of the Holy Spirit.

Romans 1:2-4

When you need a role model for living . . .

The Word became human and made his home among us. He was full of unfailing love and faithfulness. And we have seen his glory, the glory of the Father's one and only Son.

John 1:14

Christ is the visible image of the invisible God.

Colossians 1:15

JOY

When you're searching for happiness that lasts . . .

You will show me the way of life, granting me the joy of your presence and the pleasures of living with you forever.

Psalm 16:11

Those who look to him for help will be radiant with joy; no shadow of shame will darken their faces. . . . Taste and see that the LORD is good. Oh, the joys of those who take refuge in him!

Psalm 34:5, 8

How joyful are those who fear the LORD—all who follow his ways!
Psalm 128:1

When it seems there is nothing to be happy about . . .

In him our hearts rejoice, for we trust in his holy name.
Psalm 33:21

You have sorrow now, but I will see you again; then you will rejoice, and no one can rob you of that joy.
John 16:22

JUSTICE

When fighting for justice seems like a losing battle . . .

At last everyone will say, "There truly is a reward for those who live for God; surely there is a God who judges justly here on earth."
Psalm 58:11

The person who sins is the one who will die. The child will not be punished for the parent's sins, and the parent will not be punished for the child's sins. Righteous people will be rewarded for their own righteous behavior, and wicked people will be punished for their own wickedness.
Ezekiel 18:20

God blesses those who hunger and thirst for justice, for they will be satisfied.
Matthew 5:6

LIMITATIONS

When you're feeling pushed beyond your own abilities . . .

All glory to God, who is able, through his mighty power at work within us, to accomplish infinitely more than we might ask or think.

Ephesians 3:20

LIVING FOR GOD

When you want to live for God now . . .

The LORD says, "I will rescue those who love me. I will protect those who trust in my name. . . . I will reward them with a long life and give them my salvation."

Psalm 91:14, 16

My child, never forget the things I have taught you. Store my commands in your heart. If you do this, you will live many years, and your life will be satisfying.

Proverbs 3:1-2

When you're afraid of growing older . . .

O God, you have taught me from my earliest childhood, and I constantly tell others about the wonderful things you do. Now that I am old and gray, do not abandon me, O God. Let me proclaim your power to this new generation, your mighty miracles to all who come after me.

Psalm 71:17-18

I will be your God throughout your lifetime—until your hair is white with age. I made you, and I will care for you. I will carry you along and save you.
  Isaiah 46:4

LONELINESS

When you feel you have no one to turn to . . .

When you call, the LORD will answer. "Yes, I am here," he will quickly reply.
  Isaiah 58:9

When you feel as if no one cares about you . . .

How precious are your thoughts about me, O God. They cannot be numbered!
  Psalm 139:17

When you go through deep waters, I will be with you.
  Isaiah 43:2

LOVE

When you question whether anyone could ever really love you . . .

I will be glad and rejoice in your unfailing love, for you have seen my troubles, and you care about the anguish of my soul.
  Psalm 31:7

When you want to express your devotion to God . . .

Those who accept my commandments and obey them are the ones who love me. And because they love me, my Father will love them. And I will love them and reveal myself to each of them.

John 14:21

When you need to experience God's unfailing love for you . . .

No power in the sky above or in the earth below—indeed, nothing in all creation will ever be able to separate us from the love of God that is revealed in Christ Jesus our Lord.

Romans 8:39

This is real love—not that we loved God, but that he loved us and sent his Son as a sacrifice to take away our sins.

1 John 4:10

When you find it hard to love others . . .

I am giving you a new commandment: Love each other. Just as I have loved you, you should love each other. Your love for one another will prove to the world that you are my disciples.

John 13:34-35

Don't just pretend to love others. Really love them. Hate what is wrong. Hold tightly to what is good. Love each other with genuine affection, and take delight in honoring each other.

Romans 12:9-10

We love each other because he loved us first.

1 John 4:19

MARRIAGE

When you want to draw closer together . . .

Your wife will be like a fruitful grapevine, flourishing within your home. Your children will be like vigorous young olive trees as they sit around your table. That is the LORD's blessing for those who fear him.
Psalm 128:3-4

Husbands ought to love their wives as they love their own bodies. For a man who loves his wife actually shows love for himself.
Ephesians 5:28

When you start to question the benefits of your commitment to each other . . .

Two people are better off than one, for they can help each other succeed. If one person falls, the other can reach out and help. But someone who falls alone is in real trouble.
Ecclesiastes 4:9-10

Older women must train the younger women to love their husbands and their children, to live wisely and be pure, to work in their homes, to do good, and to be submissive to their husbands. Then they will not bring shame on the word of God.
Titus 2:4-5

You husbands must give honor to your wives. Treat your wife with understanding as you live together. She may be weaker than you are, but she is your equal partner in God's gift of new life. Treat her as you should so your prayers will not be hindered.

1 Peter 3:7

MERCY

When you feel like striking out against someone who has wronged you . . .

God blesses those who are merciful, for they will be shown mercy.

Matthew 5:7

When you deserve God's punishment . . .

The LORD is compassionate and merciful, slow to get angry and filled with unfailing love.

Psalm 103:8

The faithful love of the LORD never ends! His mercies never cease. Great is his faithfulness; his mercies begin afresh each morning.

Lamentations 3:22-23

MIRACLES

When others claim to be miracle workers . . .

No pagan god is like you, O Lord. None can do what you do!
Psalm 86:8

When you doubt that God has performed miracles in your life . . .

O Lord my God, you have performed many wonders for us. Your plans for us are too numerous to list. You have no equal. If I tried to recite all your wonderful deeds, I would never come to the end of them.
Psalm 40:5

When God has done the impossible in your life . . .

Come and see what our God has done, what awesome miracles he performs for people!
Psalm 66:5

MONEY

When you can barely make ends meet . . .

Seek the Kingdom of God above all else, and live righteously, and he will give you everything you need.
Matthew 6:33

When you're managing your money . . .

Don't store up treasures here on earth, where moths eat them and rust destroys them, and where thieves break in and steal. Store your treasures in heaven, where moths and rust cannot destroy, and thieves do not break in and steal. Wherever your treasure is, there the desires of your heart will also be.
Matthew 6:19-21

Give, and you will receive. Your gift will return to you in full—pressed down, shaken together to make room for more, running over, and poured into your lap. The amount you give will determine the amount you get back.
Luke 6:38

When you find yourself always wanting more . . .

Don't wear yourself out trying to get rich. Be wise enough to know when to quit. In the blink of an eye wealth disappears, for it will sprout wings and fly away like an eagle.
Proverbs 23:4-5

Those who love money will never have enough. How meaningless to think that wealth brings true happiness!
Ecclesiastes 5:10

MOTIVES

When you wonder if your motives matter to God . . .

I, the LORD, search all hearts and examine secret motives. I give all people their due rewards, according to what their actions deserve.
Jeremiah 17:10

When your actions are motivated by love for God and others . . .

Pure and genuine religion in the sight of God the Father means caring for orphans and widows in their distress and refusing to let the world corrupt you.
James 1:27

When your motives are questionable . . .

The Lord says, "These people say they are mine. They honor me with their lips, but their hearts are far from me. And their worship of me is nothing but man-made rules learned by rote." . . . What sorrow awaits those who try to hide their plans from the LORD, who do their evil deeds in the dark!
Isaiah 29:13, 15

NEEDS

When you worry about meeting your daily needs . . .

Don't worry about these things, saying, "What will we eat? What will we drink? What will we wear?" These things dominate the thoughts of unbelievers, but your heavenly Father already knows all your needs. Seek the Kingdom of God above all else, and live righteously, and he will give you everything you need.
Matthew 6:31-33

OBEDIENCE

When you doubt that God's way is best . . .

The Lord will withhold no good thing from those who do
what is right.
Psalm 84:11

Joyful are those who obey his laws and search for him with all
their hearts.
Psalm 119:2

This world is fading away, along with everything that people
crave. But anyone who does what pleases God will live forever.
1 John 2:17

When you've disobeyed God . . .

Merely listening to the law doesn't make us right with God.
It is obeying the law that makes us right in his sight.
Romans 2:13

God is working in you, giving you the desire and the power
to do what pleases him.
Philippians 2:13

When you're not sure what is the right thing to do . . .

If you look carefully into the perfect law that sets you free,
and if you do what it says and don't forget what you heard,
then God will bless you for doing it.
James 1:25

OPPORTUNITIES

When you're searching for daily opportunities from God . . .

To those who use well what they are given, even more will be given, and they will have an abundance. But from those who do nothing, even what little they have will be taken away.
  Matthew 25:29

When you're considering when to witness to others . . .

Live wisely among those who are not believers, and make the most of every opportunity. Let your conversation be gracious and attractive so that you will have the right response for everyone.
  Colossians 4:5-6

When you're waiting for just the right opportunity to come to you . . .

God is the one who provides seed for the farmer and then bread to eat. In the same way, he will provide and increase your resources and then produce a great harvest of generosity in you.
  2 Corinthians 9:10

What he opens, no one can close; and what he closes, no one can open: I know all the things you do, and I have opened a door for you that no one can close.
  Revelation 3:7-8

PATIENCE

When others get on your nerves . . .

Love is patient and kind.
  1 Corinthians 13:4

When you're being tested . . .

Patient endurance is what you need now, so that you will continue to do God's will. Then you will receive all that he has promised.
  Hebrews 10:36

God blesses those who patiently endure testing and temptation. Afterward they will receive the crown of life that God has promised to those who love him.
  James 1:12

When you feel you can't wait on God any longer . . .

I waited patiently for the Lord to help me, and he turned to me and heard my cry.
  Psalm 40:1

The Scriptures give us hope and encouragement as we wait patiently for God's promises to be fulfilled.
  Romans 15:4

PEACE

When your soul is restless . . .

You will keep in perfect peace all who trust in you, all whose thoughts are fixed on you!
Isaiah 26:3

I am leaving you with a gift—peace of mind and heart. And the peace I give is a gift the world cannot give. So don't be troubled or afraid.
John 14:27

When you need to hear words of peace rather than conflict . . .

I listen carefully to what God the LORD is saying, for he speaks peace to his faithful people.
Psalm 85:8

Those who love your instructions have great peace and do not stumble.
Psalm 119:165

This is the message of Good News for the people of Israel— that there is peace with God through Jesus Christ, who is Lord of all.
Acts 10:36

When the world around you seems at war . . .

A child is born to us, a son is given to us. The government will rest on his shoulders. And he will be called: Wonderful Counselor, Mighty God, Everlasting Father, Prince of Peace. His government and its peace will never end. He will rule with fairness and justice from the throne of his ancestor David for all eternity. The passionate commitment of the LORD of Heaven's Armies will make this happen!
   Isaiah 9:6-7

PERSECUTION

When you're oppressed for what you believe . . .

The more we suffer for Christ, the more God will shower us with his comfort through Christ.
   2 Corinthians 1:5

PERSEVERANCE

When you feel like giving up . . .

Put on every piece of God's armor so you will be able to resist the enemy in the time of evil. Then after the battle you will still be standing firm.
   Ephesians 6:13

If we are faithful to the end, trusting God just as firmly as when we first believed, we will share in all that belongs to Christ.
Hebrews 3:14

Dear brothers and sisters, when troubles come your way, consider it an opportunity for great joy. For you know that when your faith is tested, your endurance has a chance to grow. So let it grow, for when your endurance is fully developed, you will be perfect and complete, needing nothing.
James 1:2-4

POWER OF GOD

When you need supernatural strength . . .

He gives power to the weak and strength to the powerless.
Isaiah 40:29

Humanly speaking, it is impossible. But not with God. Everything is possible with God.
Mark 10:27

My grace is all you need. My power works best in weakness.
2 Corinthians 12:9

When you feel threatened by powerful people or nations . . .

All the nations you made will come and bow before you, Lord; they will praise your holy name.
Psalm 86:9

When your troubles seem too big to conquer . . .

Mightier than the violent raging of the seas, mightier than the breakers on the shore—the LORD above is mightier than these!
  Psalm 93:4

When you're tempted to take credit for the power God has given you . . .

It is not that we think we are qualified to do anything on our own. Our qualification comes from God.
  2 Corinthians 3:5

When you need a daily reminder of God's awesome power . . .

The heavens proclaim the glory of God. The skies display his craftsmanship.
  Psalm 19:1

PRAYER

When you're in distress . . .

When they call on me, I will answer; I will be with them in trouble. I will rescue and honor them.
  Psalm 91:15

I will answer them before they even call to me. While they are still talking about their needs, I will go ahead and answer their prayers!
  Isaiah 65:24

When you have a request for God . . .

If my people who are called by my name will humble themselves and pray and seek my face and turn from their wicked ways, I will hear from heaven.

2 Chronicles 7:14

Keep on asking, and you will receive what you ask for. . . . For everyone who asks, receives. . . . You parents—if your children ask for a loaf of bread, do you give them a stone instead? Or if they ask for a fish, do you give them a snake? Of course not! So if you sinful people know how to give good gifts to your children, how much more will your heavenly Father give good gifts to those who ask him.

Matthew 7:7-11

When you wonder if your prayers make a difference . . .

The earnest prayer of a righteous person has great power and produces wonderful results.

James 5:16

PRIDE

When you think your way is best . . .

Trust in the LORD with all your heart; do not depend on your own understanding. Seek his will in all you do, and he will show you which path to take. Don't be impressed with your own wisdom. Instead, fear the LORD and turn away from evil.

Proverbs 3:5-7

Humble yourselves under the mighty power of God, and at the right time he will lift you up in honor.

1 Peter 5:6

PROTECTION

When you feel vulnerable to spiritual attack . . .

If you make the LORD your refuge, if you make the Most High your shelter, no evil will conquer you.

Psalm 91:9-10

The Lord is faithful; he will strengthen you and guard you from the evil one.

2 Thessalonians 3:3

When you face physical harm . . .

The LORD . . . watches over your life. The LORD keeps watch over you as you come and go, both now and forever.

Psalm 121:7-8

PROVISION

When God has called you to a task . . .

Don't be afraid, for I am with you. Don't be discouraged, for I am your God. I will strengthen you and help you. I will hold you up with my victorious right hand.

Isaiah 41:10

By his divine power, God has given us everything we need for living a godly life.
2 Peter 1:3

When you're running out of resources . . .

This same God who takes care of me will supply all your needs from his glorious riches, which have been given to us in Christ Jesus.
Philippians 4:19

PURPOSE

When you want each moment to count . . .

I focus on this one thing: Forgetting the past and looking forward to what lies ahead, I press on to reach the end of the race and receive the heavenly prize for which God, through Christ Jesus, is calling us.
Philippians 3:13-14

When life seems so meaningless . . .

I knew you before I formed you in your mother's womb. Before you were born I set you apart.
Jeremiah 1:5

When you're feeling distracted from your purpose . . .

Turn my eyes from worthless things, and give me life through your word.
Psalm 119:37

REFRESHMENT

When you're worn out from the routine of life . . .

I long to obey your commandments! Renew my life with
your goodness.
   Psalm 119:40

The generous will prosper; those who refresh others will
themselves be refreshed.
   Proverbs 11:25

REGRETS

When you wish you had done things differently . . .

LORD, if you kept a record of our sins, who, O Lord, could
ever survive? But you offer forgiveness, that we might learn
to fear you.
   Psalm 130:3-4

Since we have been made right in God's sight by faith, we
have peace with God because of what Jesus Christ our Lord
has done for us. Because of our faith, Christ has brought us
into this place of undeserved privilege where we now stand,
and we confidently and joyfully look forward to sharing
God's glory.
   Romans 5:1-2

The kind of sorrow God wants us to experience leads us away from sin and results in salvation. There's no regret for that kind of sorrow.

2 Corinthians 7:10

Forgetting the past and looking forward to what lies ahead, I press on to reach the end of the race and receive the heavenly prize for which God, through Christ Jesus, is calling us.

Philippians 3:13-14

I will forgive their wickedness, and I will never again remember their sins.

Hebrews 8:12

RELATIONSHIPS

When your relationships seem like so much work . . .

Two people are better off than one, for they can help each other succeed. If one person falls, the other can reach out and help. But someone who falls alone is in real trouble.

Ecclesiastes 4:9-10

Take a new grip with your tired hands and strengthen your weak knees. Mark out a straight path for your feet so that those who are weak and lame will not fall but become strong.

Hebrews 12:12-13

When you have trouble finding common ground . . .

Make every effort to keep yourselves united in the Spirit, binding yourselves together with peace. For there is one body and one Spirit, just as you have been called to one glorious hope for the future. There is one Lord, one faith, one baptism, and one God and Father, who is over all and in all and living through all.

Ephesians 4:3-6

When you're searching for the joy of true friendship . . .

We can rejoice in our wonderful new relationship with God because our Lord Jesus Christ has made us friends of God.

Romans 5:11

REPENTANCE

When you've turned from God . . .

"My wayward children," says the Lord, "come back to me, and I will heal your wayward hearts."

Jeremiah 3:22

When you're truly sorry for your sins . . .

The sacrifice you desire is a broken spirit. You will not reject a broken and repentant heart, O God.

Psalm 51:17

This is a trustworthy saying, and everyone should accept it: "Christ Jesus came into the world to save sinners."
1 Timothy 1:15

If we confess our sins to him, he is faithful and just to forgive us our sins and to cleanse us from all wickedness.
1 John 1:9

REPUTATION

When you're afraid of risking your reputation by telling others about Jesus . . .

I tell you the truth, everyone who acknowledges me publicly here on earth, the Son of Man will also acknowledge in the presence of God's angels.
Luke 12:8

When you're willing to risk a good reputation for personal gain . . .

Choose a good reputation over great riches; being held in high esteem is better than silver or gold. . . . True humility and fear of the LORD lead to riches, honor, and long life.
Proverbs 22:1, 4

When others seek to destroy your reputation . . .

My child, never forget the things I have taught you. Store
my commands in your heart. If you do this, you will live
many years, and your life will be satisfying. Never let loyalty
and kindness leave you! Tie them around your neck as a
reminder. Write them deep within your heart. Then you will
find favor with both God and people, and you will earn a
good reputation.
  Proverbs 3:1-4

Humble yourselves under the mighty power of God, and at
the right time he will lift you up in honor.
  1 Peter 5:6

RESPONSIBILITY

When you need to show you're reliable . . .

To those who use well what they are given, even more
will be given, and they will have an abundance. But from
those who do nothing, even what little they have will be
taken away.
  Matthew 25:29

RESURRECTION

When you doubt Jesus actually rose from the dead . . .

"Why are your hearts filled with doubt? Look at my hands.
Look at my feet. You can see that it's really me. Touch me and
make sure that I am not a ghost, because ghosts don't have
bodies, as you see that I do." As he spoke, he showed them his
hands and his feet.
Luke 24:38-40

The Spirit of God, who raised Jesus from the dead, lives in you.
Romans 8:11

If our hope in Christ is only for this life, we are more to be
pitied than anyone in the world. But in fact, Christ has been
raised from the dead. He is the first of a great harvest of all
who have died.
1 Corinthians 15:19-20

When you wonder why the resurrection matters . . .

Since we have been made right in God's sight by the blood
of Christ, he will certainly save us from God's condemnation.
For since our friendship with God was restored by the death
of his Son while we were still his enemies, we will certainly be
saved through the life of his Son.
Romans 5:9-10

Just as death came into the world through a man, now the
resurrection from the dead has begun through another man.
Just as everyone dies because we all belong to Adam, everyone
who belongs to Christ will be given new life.
1 Corinthians 15:21-22

When you're afraid of dying . . .

I am the resurrection and the life. Anyone who believes in me will live, even after dying. Everyone who lives in me and believes in me will never ever die.
  John 11:25-26

Our bodies are buried in brokenness, but they will be raised in glory. They are buried in weakness, but they will be raised in strength. They are buried as natural human bodies, but they will be raised as spiritual bodies. For just as there are natural bodies, there are also spiritual bodies.
  1 Corinthians 15:43-44

Because God's children are human beings—made of flesh and blood—the Son also became flesh and blood. For only as a human being could he die, and only by dying could he break the power of the devil, who had the power of death. Only in this way could he set free all who have lived their lives as slaves to the fear of dying.
  Hebrews 2:14-15

SALVATION

When you need to be sure about your salvation . . .

If you confess with your mouth that Jesus is Lord and believe in your heart that God raised him from the dead, you will be saved.
  Romans 10:9

Everyone who calls on the name of the Lord will be saved.
  Joel 2:32

When you need to know the reason for your salvation . . .

God loved the world so much that he gave his one and only Son, so that everyone who believes in him will not perish but have eternal life.

John 3:16

We know that our old sinful selves were crucified with Christ so that sin might lose its power in our lives. We are no longer slaves to sin. For when we died with Christ we were set free from the power of sin.

Romans 6:6-7

You were dead because of your sins and because your sinful nature was not yet cut away. Then God made you alive with Christ, for he forgave all our sins.

Colossians 2:13

When you're wondering what happens to you inside when you're saved . . .

Through him God reconciled everything to himself. He made peace with everything in heaven and on earth by means of Christ's blood on the cross. This includes you who were once far away from God. You were his enemies, separated from him by your evil thoughts and actions. Yet now he has reconciled you to himself through the death of Christ in his physical body. As a result, he has brought you into his own presence, and you are holy and blameless as you stand before him without a single fault.

Colossians 1:20-22

When you're afraid of God's judgment . . .

Just as each person is destined to die once and after that comes judgment, so also Christ died once for all time as a sacrifice to take away the sins of many people. He will come again, not to deal with our sins, but to bring salvation to all who are eagerly waiting for him.

Hebrews 9:27-28

SICKNESS

When your health is failing . . .

I am the LORD who heals you.

Exodus 15:26

O LORD, if you heal me, I will be truly healed; if you save me, I will be truly saved. My praises are for you alone!

Jeremiah 17:14

For you who fear my name, the Sun of Righteousness will rise with healing in his wings. And you will go free, leaping with joy like calves let out to pasture.

Malachi 4:2

When you want to be spiritually healthy . . .

Do not waste time arguing over godless ideas and old wives' tales. Instead, train yourself to be godly. "Physical training is good, but training for godliness is much better, promising benefits in this life and in the life to come."

1 Timothy 4:7-8

SIN

When it seems impossible to follow God's commands . . .

Sin is no longer your master, for you no longer live under the requirements of the law. Instead, you live under the freedom of God's grace.
Romans 6:14

He personally carried our sins in his body on the cross so that we can be dead to sin and live for what is right. By his wounds you are healed.
1 Peter 2:24

If we confess our sins to him, he is faithful and just to forgive us our sins and to cleanse us from all wickedness.
1 John 1:9

When the world seems to be filled with evil . . .

Jesus gave his life for our sins, just as God our Father planned, in order to rescue us from this evil world in which we live.
Galatians 1:4

When you don't think God could forgive some of your sins . . .

He forgives all my sins and heals all my diseases. . . . He has removed our sins as far from us as the east is from the west.
Psalm 103:3, 12

Everyone who calls on the name of the LORD will be saved.

Joel 2:32

I tell you the truth, all sin and blasphemy can be forgiven, but anyone who blasphemes the Holy Spirit will never be forgiven. This is a sin with eternal consequences.

Mark 3:28-29

I am convinced that nothing can ever separate us from God's love. . . . Not even the powers of hell can separate us from God's love.

Romans 8:38

STRENGTH

When your faith is shaky . . .

The Sovereign LORD is my strength! He makes me as surefooted as a deer, able to tread upon the heights.

Habakkuk 3:19

When you're not feeling up to the task . . .

It is not by force nor by strength, but by my Spirit, says the LORD of Heaven's Armies.

Zechariah 4:6

I can do everything through Christ, who gives me strength.

Philippians 4:13

When you need the strength to keep going . . .

He gives power to the weak and strength to the powerless.
Even youths will become weak and tired, and young men will
fall in exhaustion. But those who trust in the LORD will find
new strength. They will soar high on wings like eagles. They
will run and not grow weary. They will walk and not faint.
Isaiah 40:29-31

♨ SUCCESS

When you're striving for success . . .

With God's help we will do mighty things.
Psalm 60:12

We are God's masterpiece. He has created us anew in
Christ Jesus, so we can do the good things he planned for
us long ago.
Ephesians 2:10

When you're looking for the key to success in God's eyes . . .

I tell you the truth, anyone who believes in me will do the
same works I have done, and even greater works, because I am
going to be with the Father.
John 14:12

SUFFERING

When the pain is unbearable . . .

The LORD is close to the brokenhearted; he rescues those whose spirits are crushed. The righteous person faces many troubles, but the LORD comes to the rescue each time.
  Psalm 34:18-19

The more we suffer for Christ, the more God will shower us with his comfort through Christ.
  2 Corinthians 1:5

When you need comfort from someone who understands . . .

In all their suffering he also suffered, and he personally rescued them. In his love and mercy he redeemed them. He lifted them up and carried them through all the years.
  Isaiah 63:9

All praise to God, the Father of our Lord Jesus Christ. God is our merciful Father and the source of all comfort. He comforts us in all our troubles so that we can comfort others. When they are troubled, we will be able to give them the same comfort God has given us.
  2 Corinthians 1:3-4

When you need the courage to endure . . .

Sing for joy, O heavens! Rejoice, O earth! Burst into song, O mountains! For the LORD has comforted his people and will have compassion on them in their suffering.
  Isaiah 49:13

Don't be afraid of what you are about to suffer. . . . If you remain faithful even when facing death, I will give you the crown of life.
  Revelation 2:10

TEMPTATION

When doing the wrong thing seems like more fun . . .

The path of the virtuous leads away from evil; whoever follows that path is safe.
  Proverbs 16:17

Temptation comes from our own desires, which entice us and drag us away. These desires give birth to sinful actions. And when sin is allowed to grow, it gives birth to death.
  James 1:14-15

When you feel like you can't resist . . .

The temptations in your life are no different from what others experience. And God is faithful. He will not allow the temptation to be more than you can stand. When you are tempted, he will show you a way out so that you can endure.
  1 Corinthians 10:13

THOUGHTS

When you want to control your thoughts . . .

You will keep in perfect peace all who trust in you, all whose thoughts are fixed on you!

Isaiah 26:3

Supplement your faith with a generous provision of . . . knowledge with self-control, and self-control with patient endurance, and patient endurance with godliness.

2 Peter 1:5-6

When temptation threatens godly thoughts . . .

Those who are dominated by the sinful nature think about sinful things, but those who are controlled by the Holy Spirit think about things that please the Spirit. So letting your sinful nature control your mind leads to death. But letting the Spirit control your mind leads to life and peace.

Romans 8:5-6

TROUBLED TIMES

When you face tragedy . . .

God is our refuge and strength, always ready to help in times of trouble. So we will not fear when earthquakes come and the mountains crumble into the sea.

Psalm 46:1-2

When your problems seem to pile up . . .

Our present troubles are small and won't last very long. Yet they produce for us a glory that vastly outweighs them and will last forever!

2 Corinthians 4:17

When you need supernatural peace in times of crisis . . .

I have told you all this so that you may have peace in me. Here on earth you will have many trials and sorrows. But take heart, because I have overcome the world.

John 16:33

When you need someone to call for help . . .

The righteous person faces many troubles, but the LORD comes to the rescue each time.

Psalm 34:19

I will call to you whenever I'm in trouble, and you will answer me.

Psalm 86:7

TRUSTING GOD

When there is no one you can count on . . .

Let us hold tightly without wavering to the hope we affirm, for God can be trusted to keep his promise.

Hebrews 10:23

When you give God control of your life . . .

Blessed are those who trust in the LORD and have made the LORD their hope and confidence. They are like trees planted along a riverbank, with roots that reach deep into the water. Such trees are not bothered by the heat or worried by long months of drought. Their leaves stay green, and they never stop producing fruit.
Jeremiah 17:7-8

When you question why you should trust God . . .

O LORD of Heaven's Armies, what joy for those who trust in you.
Psalm 84:12

The LORD is good, a strong refuge when trouble comes. He is close to those who trust in him.
Nahum 1:7

If we are faithful to the end, trusting God just as firmly as when we first believed, we will share in all that belongs to Christ.
Hebrews 3:14

VICTORY

When you need a spiritual victory . . .

Victory comes from you, O LORD. May you bless your people.
Psalm 3:8

You belong to God, my dear children. You have already won a victory over those people, because the Spirit who lives in you is greater than the spirit who lives in the world.

1 John 4:4

When you feel like a loser . . .

The LORD is my strength and my song; he has given me victory. This is my God, and I will praise him—my father's God, and I will exalt him!

Exodus 15:2

Look, I have given you authority over all the power of the enemy, and you can walk among snakes and scorpions and crush them. Nothing will injure you.

Luke 10:19

Every child of God defeats this evil world, and we achieve this victory through our faith. And who can win this battle against the world? Only those who believe that Jesus is the Son of God.

1 John 5:4-5

WEARINESS

When life moves so fast you can't slow down . . .

He gives power to the weak and strength to the powerless. Even youths will become weak and tired, and young men will fall in exhaustion. But those who trust in the LORD will find new strength. They will soar high on wings like eagles. They will run and not grow weary. They will walk and not faint.

Isaiah 40:29-31

When your soul is weary . . .

I have given rest to the weary and joy to the sorrowing.
  Jeremiah 31:25

Come to me, all of you who are weary and carry heavy
burdens, and I will give you rest. Take my yoke upon you. Let
me teach you, because I am humble and gentle at heart, and
you will find rest for your souls.
  Matthew 11:28-29

WILL OF GOD

When you feel removed from God's plans . . .

I will guide you along the best pathway for your life. I will
advise you and watch over you.
  Psalm 32:8

Don't copy the behavior and customs of this world, but let
God transform you into a new person by changing the way
you think. Then you will learn to know God's will for you,
which is good and pleasing and perfect.
  Romans 12:2

When you want to be faithful to God's plan each day . . .

You will be accepted if you do what is right. But if you refuse
to do what is right, then watch out! Sin is crouching at the
door, eager to control you. But you must subdue it and be
its master.
  Genesis 4:7

The LORD directs the steps of the godly. He delights in every detail of their lives.
  Psalm 37:23

When you question God's ultimate design . . .

"I know the plans I have for you," says the LORD. "They are plans for good and not for disaster, to give you a future and a hope."
  Jeremiah 29:11

WISDOM

When you need to discern God's will and ways . . .

Fear of the LORD is the foundation of true wisdom. All who obey his commandments will grow in wisdom.
  Psalm 111:10

Knowledge of the Holy One results in good judgment.
  Proverbs 9:10

If you need wisdom, ask our generous God, and he will give it to you. He will not rebuke you for asking.
  James 1:5

When you seek to understand God, your Creator . . .

You will understand what it means to fear the LORD, and you will gain knowledge of God. For the LORD grants wisdom! From his mouth come knowledge and understanding.
  Proverbs 2:5-6

WORD OF GOD

When you question the relevance of God's Word today . . .

The rain and snow come down from the heavens and stay on the ground to water the earth. They cause the grain to grow, producing seed for the farmer and bread for the hungry. It is the same with my word. I send it out, and it always produces fruit. It will accomplish all I want it to, and it will prosper everywhere I send it.

   Isaiah 55:10-11

All Scripture is inspired by God and is useful to teach us what is true and to make us realize what is wrong in our lives. It corrects us when we are wrong and teaches us to do what is right. God uses it to prepare and equip his people to do every good work.

   2 Timothy 3:16-17

When you need wisdom directly from God . . .

Your laws please me; they give me wise advice.

   Psalm 119:24

Your word is a lamp to guide my feet and a light for my path.

   Psalm 119:105

When you need to hear the truth . . .

The grass withers and the flowers fade, but the word of our God stands forever.

   Isaiah 40:8

You have been born again, but not to a life that will quickly end. Your new life will last forever because it comes from the eternal, living word of God. As the Scriptures say, "People are like grass; their beauty is like a flower in the field. The grass withers and the flower fades. But the word of the Lord remains forever." And that word is the Good News that was preached to you.

1 Peter 1:23-25

WORK

When you're unhappy at your job . . .

My dear brothers and sisters, be strong and immovable. Always work enthusiastically for the Lord, for you know that nothing you do for the Lord is ever useless.

1 Corinthians 15:58

Pay careful attention to your own work, for then you will get the satisfaction of a job well done, and you won't need to compare yourself to anyone else. For we are each responsible for our own conduct.

Galatians 6:4-5

When you're overworked . . .

There is a special rest still waiting for the people of God. For all who have entered into God's rest have rested from their labors, just as God did after creating the world.

Hebrews 4:9-10

When your boss is hard to work with . . .

Work willingly at whatever you do, as though you were working for the Lord rather than for people. Remember that the Lord will give you an inheritance as your reward, and that the Master you are serving is Christ.

Colossians 3:23-24

WORRY

When you can't get rid of those anxious feelings . . .

Don't worry about these things, saying, "What will we eat? What will we drink? What will we wear?" These things dominate the thoughts of unbelievers, but your heavenly Father already knows all your needs.

Matthew 6:31-32

Don't worry about anything; instead, pray about everything. Tell God what you need, and thank him for all he has done. Then you will experience God's peace, which exceeds anything we can understand. His peace will guard your hearts and minds as you live in Christ Jesus.

Philippians 4:6-7

Give all your worries and cares to God, for he cares about you.

1 Peter 5:7

WORSHIP

When you need to draw close to God . . .

If my people who are called by my name will humble themselves and pray and seek my face and turn from their wicked ways, I will hear from heaven and will forgive their sins and restore their land.
2 Chronicles 7:14

When he prays to God, he will be accepted. And God will receive him with joy and restore him to good standing.
Job 33:26

Let us go right into the presence of God with sincere hearts fully trusting him. For our guilty consciences have been sprinkled with Christ's blood to make us clean, and our bodies have been washed with pure water.
Hebrews 10:22

Come close to God, and God will come close to you.
James 4:8

When you long to express your heart to God . . .

As the deer longs for streams of water, so I long for you, O God. I thirst for God, the living God.
Psalm 42:1-2

It is good to give thanks to the LORD, to sing praises to the Most High.
Psalm 92:1

When you desire to honor God, in recognition of who he is . . .

Come, let us worship and bow down. Let us kneel before the LORD our maker, for he is our God. We are the people he watches over, the flock under his care.
  Psalm 95:6-7

When you desire to honor God for what he's done for you . . .

The LORD is my strength and my song; he has given me victory. This is my God, and I will praise him—my father's God, and I will exalt him!
  Exodus 15:2

Praise the LORD, for he has shown me the wonders of his unfailing love.
  Psalm 31:21

May the Lord Bless You

May the LORD bless you and protect you. May the LORD smile on you and be gracious to you. May the LORD show you his favor and give you his peace.

Numbers 6:24-26

The Lord Is with You

Be strong and courageous! Do not be afraid and do not panic before them. For the LORD your God will personally go ahead of you. He will neither fail you nor abandon you.

Deuteronomy 31:6

Perfect Peace

In peace I will lie down and sleep, for you alone, O LORD, will keep me safe.

Psalm 4:8

The Shepherd's Psalm

The LORD is my shepherd; I have all that I need. He lets me rest in green meadows; he leads me beside peaceful streams. He renews my strength. He guides me along right paths, bringing honor to his name. Even when I walk through the darkest valley, I will not be afraid, for you are close beside me. Your rod and your staff protect and comfort me. You prepare a feast for me in the presence of my enemies. You honor me by anointing my head with oil. My cup overflows with blessings. Surely your goodness and unfailing love will pursue me all the days of my life, and I will live in the house of the LORD forever.

Psalm 23:1-6

The Lord Cares for You

You are my hiding place; you protect me from trouble. You surround me with songs of victory.

Psalm 32:7

The Lord Is Near

The LORD hears his people when they call to him for help. He rescues them from all their troubles. The LORD is close to the brokenhearted; he rescues those whose spirits are crushed. The righteous person faces many troubles, but the LORD comes to the rescue each time.

Psalm 34:17-19

The Lord Encourages

I waited patiently for the LORD to help me, and he turned to me and heard my cry. He lifted me out of the pit of despair, out of the mud and the mire. He set my feet on solid ground and steadied me as I walked along. He has given me a new song to sing, a hymn of praise to our God. Many will see what he has done and be amazed. They will put their trust in the LORD.

Psalm 40:1-3

The Lord Is Your Help

Why am I discouraged? Why is my heart so sad? I will put my hope in God! I will praise him again—my Savior and my God!

Psalm 42:11

Give Thanks

Give thanks to the LORD, for he is good! *His faithful love endures forever.* Give thanks to the God of gods. *His faithful love endures forever.* Give thanks to the Lord of lords. *His faithful love endures forever.* Give thanks to him who alone does mighty miracles. *His faithful love endures forever.* Give thanks to him who made the heavens so skillfully. *His faithful love endures forever.*

Psalm 136:1-5

The Lord Watches over You

You know when I sit down or stand up. You know my thoughts even when I'm far away. You see me when I travel and when I rest at home. You know everything I do.

Psalm 139:2-3

Trust in the Lord

You will keep in perfect peace all who trust in you, all whose thoughts are fixed on you! Trust in the LORD always, for the LORD GOD is the eternal Rock.

Isaiah 26:3-4

Do Not Be Afraid

Don't be afraid, for I am with you. Don't be discouraged, for I am your God. I will strengthen you and help you. I will hold you up with my victorious right hand.

Isaiah 41:10

The Lord Is Merciful

"The mountains may move and the hills disappear, but even then my faithful love for you will remain. My covenant of blessing will never be broken," says the LORD, who has mercy on you.

Isaiah 54:10

The Lord Is My Strength

Even though the fig trees have no blossoms, and there are no grapes on the vines; even though the olive crop fails, and the fields lie empty and barren; even though the flocks die in the fields, and the cattle barns are empty, yet I will rejoice in the LORD! I will be joyful in the God of my salvation! The Sovereign LORD is my strength! He makes me as surefooted as a deer, able to tread upon the heights.

Habakkuk 3:17-19

The Lord Helps the Weak

It is not by force nor by strength, but by my Spirit, says the
LORD of Heaven's Armies.
   Zechariah 4:6

The Beatitudes

God blesses those who are poor and realize their need for
him, for the Kingdom of Heaven is theirs. God blesses those
who mourn, for they will be comforted. God blesses those
who are humble, for they will inherit the whole earth. God
blesses those who hunger and thirst for justice, for they will
be satisfied. God blesses those who are merciful, for they will
be shown mercy. God blesses those whose hearts are pure, for
they will see God. God blesses those who work for peace, for
they will be called the children of God. God blesses those who
are persecuted for doing right, for the Kingdom of Heaven is
theirs. God blesses you when people mock you and persecute
you and lie about you and say all sorts of evil things against
you because you are my followers. Be happy about it! Be very
glad! For a great reward awaits you in heaven. And remember,
the ancient prophets were persecuted in the same way.
   Matthew 5:3-12

Jesus Gives Rest

Come to me, all of you who are weary and carry heavy
burdens, and I will give you rest. Take my yoke upon you. Let
me teach you, because I am humble and gentle at heart, and
you will find rest for your souls. For my yoke is easy to bear,
and the burden I give you is light.
   Matthew 11:28-30

God Gives Eternal Life

The wages of sin is death, but the free gift of God is eternal life through Christ Jesus our Lord.

Romans 6:23

God Works for Our Good

We know that God causes everything to work together for the good of those who love God and are called according to his purpose for them.

Romans 8:28

No One Can Oppose God

What shall we say about such wonderful things as these? If God is for us, who can ever be against us? Since he did not spare even his own Son but gave him up for us all, won't he also give us everything else?

Romans 8:31-32

Nothing Can Separate Us from God's Love

Nothing can ever separate us from God's love. Neither death nor life, neither angels nor demons, neither our fears for today nor our worries about tomorrow—not even the powers of hell can separate us from God's love. No power in the sky above or in the earth below—indeed, nothing in all creation will ever be able to separate us from the love of God that is revealed in Christ Jesus our Lord.

Romans 8:38-39

Christ's Love

Christ will make his home in your hearts as you trust in him. Your roots will grow down into God's love and keep you strong. And may you have the power to understand, as all God's people should, how wide, how long, how high, and how deep his love is. May you experience the love of Christ, though it is too great to understand fully. Then you will be made complete with all the fullness of life and power that comes from God.

Ephesians 3:17-19

Go to God in Time of Need

Let us come boldly to the throne of our gracious God. There we will receive his mercy, and we will find grace to help us when we need it most.

Hebrews 4:16

The Lord Is Our Helper

We can say with confidence, "The LORD is my helper, so I will have no fear. What can mere people do to me?"

Hebrews 13:6

The Lord Never Changes

Jesus Christ is the same yesterday, today, and forever.

Hebrews 13:8